BEER

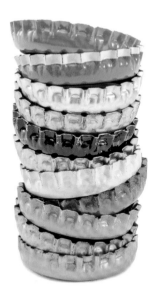

BEER

150
AWESOME FACTS
ABOUT YOUR
FAVORITE
BREW

CAROLINE WEST

DOG 'n' BONE

Published in 2018 by Dog 'n' Bone Books
An imprint of Ryland Peters & Small Ltd
20–21 Jockey's Fields   341 E 116th St
London WC1R 4BW   New York, NY 10029

www.rylandpeters.com

10 9 8 7 6 5 4 3 2 1

A CIP catalog record for this book is available from
the Library of Congress and the British Library.

ISBN: 978 1 911026 67 9

Printed in China

Editor: *Caroline West*
Designer: *Mark Latter*

Contents

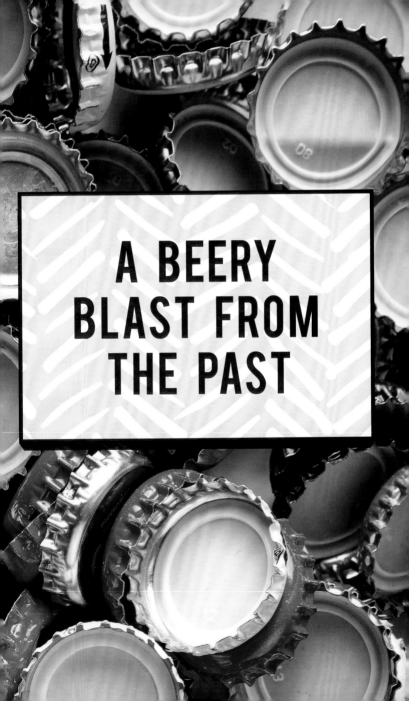

A BEERY BLAST FROM THE PAST

Beer is one of the world's oldest alcoholic beverages. Chemical evidence of barley beer dates back to around 3400–3000 BCE, having been found at the ancient Sumerian settlement at Godin Tepe, in the central Zagros Mountains of Iran.

In the ancient past, women brewed beer at home. The beer was not quite like the libation we know and love today—being used as a food supplement, it was thick, porridge-like, and drunk through a straw.

The Ancient Egyptians believed that Osiris, one of their most important gods, was responsible for teaching humans how to make beer.

In Babylon, 4,000 years ago, a bride's father would supply his son-in-law with all the mead (honey beer) that he could drink for a month after the wedding. Since the Babylonian calendar was based on the lunar cycle, this period became known as a "honey month" or what we now refer to as a "honeymoon."

Hops were not used to flavor ancient beers; instead, brewers would use plants such as mugwort, heather, wild carrot, henbane, and elderberry, ingredients that were also used centuries later by medieval brewers.

An early Mesopotamian stone tablet from around 1800 BCE is inscribed with the *Hymn to Ninkasi* (the Sumerian goddess of beer). This poem contains the oldest known written recipe for beer.

Dr. Patrick E. McGovern of the University of Pennsylvania, an expert on ancient fermented beverages, collaborated with Dogfish Head Brewery, in Delaware, USA, to create a beer from the deep and distant past. Using archaeological evidence found at a Neolithic burial site in northern China, they replicated a 9,000-year-old alcoholic brew that contained rice, grapes, hawthorn berries, and honey. Released in 2006, only 3,000 cases of the Chateau Jiahu beer were produced.

Archaeologists from the University of Chicago and brewers from Anchor Brewing, in San Francisco, USA, joined forces to create the beer described in the *Hymn to Ninkasi* (see opposite). Using replicas of ancient tools and ceramic fermentation pots, barley that had been malted on a roof, and yeast similar to the type used in the ancient past, the team created a beer that tasted very similar to hard apple cider, with an ABV of 3.5%.

Brewers from the former Scottish & Newcastle brewery, in Edinburgh, UK, attempted to recreate an ancient Egyptian beer in association with researchers from Cambridge University, who were excavating the ancient workers' village at Amarna in Egypt. This had been destroyed by the Egyptian pharaoh Tutankhamun in around 1300 BCE. The limited-release Tutankhamun Ale was sold in a wooden box modeled on crates used by Howard Carter, the archaeologist who excavated Tutankhamun's tomb in the early 20th century.

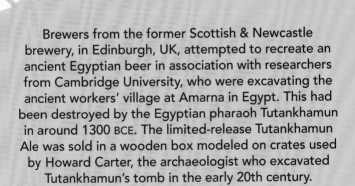

The Ancient Egyptians built the pyramids with the help of beer, with workers at the famous Giza Plateau receiving a substantial daily ration of beer for their toils in the hot sun.

The Greeks and Romans famously preferred wine to beer; th Romans associating beer-drinking with the barbarian horde of Northern Europe. In fact, the Roman Emperor Julian eve went so far as to describe beer as smelling like a billy goat

One of the edicts in the *Code of Hammurabi* (c. 1750 BCE), laid down by the Ancient Babylonian King Hammurabi, stated that any brewer or tavern owner caught diluting beer or using low-quality grains to improve profits would face the death penalty—by being drowned in the offending beer.

TOP 10
Beer-Guzzling Nations

1 Czech Republic *143.3 liters*

2 Namibia *108 liters*

3 Austria *106 liters*

4 Germany *104.2 liters*

5 Poland *100.8 liters*

6 Ireland *98.2 liters*

7 Romania *94.1 liters*

8 Seychelles *90.0 liters*

9 Estonia *89.5 liters*

10 Lithuania *88.7 liters*

[AVERAGE ANNUAL BEER CONSUMPTION IN 2016 IN LITERS PER CAPITA]

TOP 5
Beer-Consuming Countries

1 China *41.772 billion liters*

2 United States *24.245 billion liters*

3 Brazil *12.654 billion liters*

4 Germany *8.412 billion liters*

5 Russia *8.405 billion liters*

[TOTAL ANNUAL BEER CONSUMPTION
IN 2016 IN LITERS PER COUNTRY]

Beer soup was common in medieval and early modern Europe. Although recipes and additional flavorings varied, the basic recipe called for a dark brown beer, cream, fat, and flour or egg yolk. Form an orderly queue now...

It has been suggested that, after consuming a pail or two of the intoxicating brew which they called *aul*, or ale, Vikings would go valiantly into battle, often without armor or even shirts. In fact, berserk means "bare shirt" in Old Norse and the fearless Viking warriors became known as berserkers.

The first recorded use of hops for brewing was in 822 CE when Abbot Adalhard of the Benedictine monastery in Corbie, Picardy, France, included instructions on the use of wild hops when making beer in a set of rules for the monastery.

The Vikings were under the bizarre impression that they would be greeted in Valhalla, their heaven, by a giant goat whose udders could provide endless supplies of beer.

Monks in the Middle Ages believed that the mortar used to build churches and monasteries was stronger if it was mixed with ale rather than water.

During the Middle Ages, the monks at European monasteries became expert brewers. In those days, it was safer to drink beer rather than water because the brewing process provided sterilization, as well as additional nutrients. Based on a system developed in about 800 CE at the Abbey of Saint Gall, a monastery in Switzerland, monastic breweries would run three breweries: one to brew for customers, one for the monks' beer, and one to make free beer for the poor.

The first professional brewers during the Middle Ages were women; they were known as ale wives or brewsters.

Brewing goes back a long way, but the oldest brewery still pumping out beer today is Weihenstephan, near Munich, Germany, which was originally founded in 1040.

According to *Guinness World Records*, The Bingley Arms, in Bardsey, Leeds, UK, is the world's oldest pub, dating back to 953 CE (although evidence suggests that it might even go back as far as 905 CE).

The *Kalevala*, a set of ancient epic Finnish folk songs collected for publication in 1835 by Elias Lönnrot, describes the boiling of "barley, hops, and water" to "steep, and seethe, and bubble" in order to make intoxicating beer.

Before the invention of thermometers, brewers would dip a thumb or finger in the wort to check it was the right temperature before adding the yeast to kick-start fermentation. Too cold, and the yeast wouldn't grow; too hot, and the yeast would die—hence, the phrase "rule of thumb."

In 1516, Duke Wilhelm IV of Bavaria introduced the Reinheitsgebot (German Beer Purity Law), stipulating that beer was to contain just three ingredients: water, barley, and hops.

In English pubs, ale is ordered in pints and quarts. So in days gone by, if customers got a little unruly, the bartender would yell at them to mind their pints and quarts, and settle down. It's where we get the phrase "mind your Ps and Qs."

During the 1200s, it was acceptable to baptize babies in beer—until Pope Gregory IX intervened and decreed that such baptisms were invalid.

THE NEW WORLD

In 1620, the Pilgrim Fathers embarked on an epic journey on the *Mayflower* across the Atlantic Ocean to found the first colony in New England, USA. According to a diary entry made by one passenger, the pilgrims were forced to disembark at Plymouth Rock, instead of Virginia, because the crew onboard the rented ship were concerned that they would run out of beer for the return journey to England.

Thomas Jefferson, one of the Founding Fathers of the United States, wrote a draft of the Declaration of Independence in the Indian Queen tavern in Philadelphia, apparently while sipping on ale.

The flag that inspired Francis Scott Key to pen *The Star-Spangled Banner*, the national anthem of the United States, was stitched by flag-maker Mary Pickersgill on the floor of a brewery in Baltimore. The finished flag measured 42 x 30ft (13 x 9m), so Mary needed a large space where she could work on her hands and knees.

Ancient Inca girls, aged around 8–10 years old, would chew corn into a pulp-like consistency, and then spit it into large vats of warm water where it would sit and ferment for several weeks. The lumpy, spit-filled beer would then be strained for drinking.

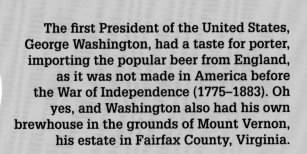

The first President of the United States, George Washington, had a taste for porter, importing the popular beer from England, as it was not made in America before the War of Independence (1775–1883). Oh yes, and Washington also had his own brewhouse in the grounds of Mount Vernon, his estate in Fairfax County, Virginia.

Nursing mothers and wet nurses in mid-19th-century Munich, Germany, aimed to drink up to 7 pints of beer a day, believing this was necessary for successful breastfeeding. Fools! In 1876, Munich's health department made it clear that 2 pints was the recommended dose.

During World War One, the Chancellor of the Exchequer, David Lloyd George, led a campaign to persuade people to consume less alcohol in the belief that excess drinking was affecting the war effort. When this had little effect, the British Government introduced a "No Treating Order," which stated that any drink had to be consumed only by the person paying for it. The maximum penalty for buying a round of drinks for other people was six months in prison.

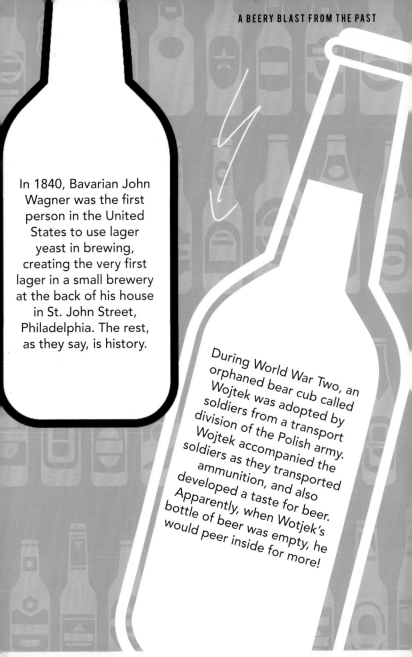

In 1840, Bavarian John Wagner was the first person in the United States to use lager yeast in brewing, creating the very first lager in a small brewery at the back of his house in St. John Street, Philadelphia. The rest, as they say, is history.

During World War Two, an orphaned bear cub called Wojtek was adopted by soldiers from a transport division of the Polish army. Wojtek accompanied the soldiers as they transported ammunition, and also developed a taste for beer. Apparently, when Wotjek's bottle of beer was empty, he would peer inside for more!

Prohibition

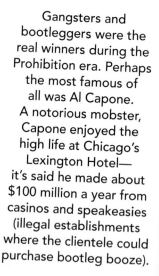

The Volstead Act gave the federal authorities in the US the power to stop the production, sale, or importation of "intoxicating liquor." Prohibition began on January 16, 1920, and ended on December 5, 1933. That's 13 years, 10 months, 19 days, 17 hours, and 32½ minutes—what a long wait for a cold beer!

Gangsters and bootleggers were the real winners during the Prohibition era. Perhaps the most famous of all was Al Capone. A notorious mobster, Capone enjoyed the high life at Chicago's Lexington Hotel—it's said he made about $100 million a year from casinos and speakeasies (illegal establishments where the clientele could purchase bootleg booze).

Franklin D. Roosevelt, 32nd President of the United States, was first inaugurated in March 1933. When Prohibition ended, he is purported to have said: *"What America needs now is a drink."*

Thousands of barrels of booze, including beer, were poured into rivers or burned as a result of Prohibition. On May 19, 1925, at an army base in Brooklyn, 10,000 barrels of beer were poured into New York Harbor.

Temperance advocate, Carry Nation campaigned tirelessly to bring in Prohibition. Her methods were determined, to say the least, including serenading patrons drinking in saloons in Kansas, and smashing bars with hatchets and rocks. During these exploits, Carry was often accompanied by hymn-singing women. She was arrested over 30 times during her anti-drinking campaign, but sold souvenir hatchets to pay her fines.

Support for Prohibition gradually ebbed away, not that it had ever been that popular. Newspaper articles of the time suggest that up to 8 out of 10 congressmen were secret drinkers anyway.

BEER
TRIVIA

FUN AND FASCINATING BEER FACTS

Zythology is the official name for the study of beer and beer-making. It is derived from the Greek words *zythos* (meaning "beer") and *logos* (meaning "study").

The word beer may come from the Latin *bibere*, meaning "to drink or toast." Some experts believe it might also originate from the Proto-Germanic word *beuwoz*. Over the centuries, variations developed, with the Old English using *beor* and the Germans saying *bier*. Cheers, anyway!

Saint Brigid of Ireland (d.525 CE) is said to have performed miracles, including changing water into beer for a leper colony and supplying enough beer for 18 churches from a single barrel. Oh yes, and she's also one of the patron saints of beer.

After winning the Nobel Prize for Physics in 1922, Danish scientist Niels Bohr was rewarded by the Carlsberg brewery with a house and a limitless supply of piped beer. The pipe ran from the brewery directly to Niels' house.

After water and tea, beer is the most popular drink in the world.

You can use beer to shine up copper kettles, as a hair conditioner, and to soften/tenderize meat—it's not just for drinking!

Salvage divers uncovered the oldest drinkable beer in the world in 2010, while investigating an early 19th-century shipwreck in the Baltic Sea. The beer in the bottles had been preserved because the culture in the beer was still alive.

Portland, in Oregon, USA, has many nicknames, one of which is "Beervana" due to the large number of microbreweries in the region.

Every April, at the start of Bavarian Beer Week, in Munich, Germany, an open-air beer fountain dispenses free beer to the public.

Beer commercials in the USA are not allowed to show people *actually* drinking beer. US television networks have regulations stating that people cannot be shown consuming an alcoholic beverage in any TV commercial.

Before hops became a key ingredient in brewing, brewers used gruit, a mixture of herbs and spices such as bog myrtle, yarrow, aniseed, juniper, and nutmeg to make beer bitter and add flavor. Some modern craft breweries are now creating gruit ales and gather at International Gruit Day each year to celebrate this ancient style of beer-making.

Six-packs of beer first became commercially available in the late 1940s, with Pabst Brewing usually being credited as the first brewer to package beer in this way—either because a six-pack was considered the ideal weight for the average person to carry or because it would fit into a standard grocery bag.

In 1952, novelist Ernest Hemingway appeared in an advertisement for Ballantine Ale, one of America's bestselling beers at the time.

Australian brewery James Squire created a limited-release, porter-style ale from yeast discovered in bottles of beer on a 220-year-old shipwreck. In 1797, *Sydney Cove*, a ship carrying tea, tobacco, and rice, as well as wine, port, beer, and spirits from Calcutta to Sydney, sank off the coast of Preservation Island, north-east of Tasmania. At the time of writing, *The Wreck Preservation Ale* is only available for a short time, in May and June 2018.

A government-funded project in 2013 saw the city of Amsterdam pay alcoholics in beer to clean the streets. For every day that they turned up for work, the alcoholics would get 10 euros, five cans of beer, and half a pouch of tobacco.

In popular culture, people who collect beer-bottle labels are known as labeorphilists.

Meadophily is the study of beer-bottle labels.

Collecting beer mats or coasters as a hobby has a special name—tegestology.

Jim Whitaker became the first American to reach the summit of Mount Everest on May 1, 1963, taking a can of Rainier Beer with him, of course.

A 4-mile (6.5-km) underground pipeline supplied 105,668 US gallons (400,000 liters) of lager to heavy-metal music lovers at the 2017 Wacken Open Air Show, in Schleswig-Holstein, Germany. Bartenders were able to serve the metalheads at a rate of six lagers per second.

In the past, people drank weak beer to avoid the impurities in water. Young children, who were no longer breastfeeding, also drank beer. Understandably, this made them slightly unsteady on their feet, hence the term "toddlers."

The Jelly Belly Candy Company sells beer-flavored jelly beans in a novelty beer can—please note: they are nonalcoholic.

The short-lived Beer Lovers' Party of Belarus, near Russia, was registered on December 30, 1993. The political party's logo was a plump hedgehog holding a flag and a tankard of beer.

Go to a traditional beer house in the Czech Republic and the bartender will keep refilling your glass unless you place a coaster on top to indicate that you've had enough for one night!

There is a crater on the moon called Beer, which is named after German astronomer Wilhelm Wolff Beer.

The world's oldest trademark belongs to Bass Brewery. Bass's distinctive red triangle was the first registered trademark issued by the British government in 1876. The logo became so popular that it even features on a bottle in Impressionist painter Édouard Manet's work "A Bar at the Folies-Bergère."

Porcupine Quill Brewing, in KwaZulu-Natal, South Africa, took its name from the discovery of two porcupines in the spot where the microbrewery is now located.

Death By Beer

On October 17, 1814, nearly 400,000 US gallons (1,470,000 liters) of beer burst from vats at the Meux and Company Brewery in Tottenham Court Road, London, causing a tidal wave of beer. Two houses were destroyed and eight people died.

In the past, brewery workers faced many hazards, including drowning in beer and the inhalation of carbon dioxide emitted from open fermenters. Here are just a few of the gruesome ends met by these heroic beer-making men:

In 1903, George Castle, a cellar-man who worked for the Walkerville Brewery, in Adelaide, Australia, drowned in a large vat of stout, being overcome by the carbon-dioxide fumes before falling and drowning in the beer.

A poor chap called Edmond from New Zealand met his death in a vat of beer in 1932. This time, the drowning was deliberate, as he left a note, saying: "You'll find me in No.3. Cheerio to all."

Still worse, some brewery workers were scalded to death—for example, in 1900, James Kirby, who worked for the Esk Brewery, in Launceston, UK, died after falling into a vat of boiling mash nearly 10ft (3m) deep. Sadly, Kirby's hat was later found floating in the vat.

WEIRD AND WACKY BEER FACTS

Cenosillicaphobia is the fear of an empty glass.

We all know we should recycle as much as possible, right? Well, Wat Larn Kuad, a Buddhist temple, in rural Sisaket, Thailand, is built with over one million recycled beer bottles.

Every year, the town of Sonkäjarvi, in Finland, hosts its famous Wife Carrying World Championships. The winner of the contest receives a very special prize—his wife's weight in beer.

Quite a novelty this one. Rogue Ales, in Newport, Oregon, USA, make a rather unusual beer. Their Beard Beer is brewed with wild yeast cultivated from the beard of brewmaster John Maier. John has had his beard since 1978!

Texas state law forbids a person from taking more than three sips of beer while standing up.

The winner of the "Most Creative Fried Food" at the Texas State Fair of 2010 was, wait for it, Fried Beer Ravioli. This culinary delight entailed deep-frying ravioli made from a pretzel-like dough filled with beer.

The law states that bars in Australia must provide stabling, water, and food for horses belonging to patrons.

In the early 1990s, The Trading Post, in Lajitas, Texas, USA, was home to a beer-swilling goat called Clay Henry Sr. Customers would line up to give the black mountain goat a beer. Clay would hold the bottle in his mouth and swig back the beer unaided. Sadly, Clay passed away in 1992, although his son, Clay Henry Jr., was also partial to a beer or two.

In Nebraska, USA, bars that serve beer have to be cooking a kettle of soup at the same time.

In Arvada, Colorado, USA, premises licensed to sell alcohol—and that includes beer—are required by law to provide enough lighting for someone to be able to read inside.

Everybody loves Hello Kitty, right? Well, in 2013, Taiwanese beer producer Long Quan produced Hello Kitty Beer in four delicious fruit flavors and packaged it in cute and colorful cans. The low alcohol content (at 2.3–2.8% ABV) was designed to appeal to Chinese women.

The *Encyclopedia Britannia* was once banned in Texas because it contained a recipe for making beer that people could use at home.

In the city of St. Louis, Missouri, USA, it is illegal to sit on the curb of any street while drinking beer from a pail. Darn it!

TOP 10
Low-Calorie Beers

1 Budweiser Select 55
55 calories

2 Beck's Premier Light
64 calories
Miller 64
64 calories

3 Bikini Beer
80 calories

4 Michelob Ultra
Pure Gold
85 calories

5 Amstel Extra Light
90 calories

6 Michelob Ultra
95 calories
Natural Light
95 calories
Busch Light
95 calories

7 Yuengling Light Lager
99 calories
Corona Light
99 calories
Heineken Premium
Light
99 calories

8 Keystone Light
101 calories

9 Coors Light
102 calories

10 Bud Light
110 calories

[NUMBER OF CALORIES PER 12 USFL OZ (355ML) SERVING]

Weird Beer Ingredients

Brewers put some odd ingredients in beer, although usually with very good reason. Check out this sample of wonderful brews:

Cigar City's *Cucumber Saison* is a special-release beer containing, you guessed it, cucumber. This refreshing ale has notes of honey, tropical fruit, bitter lemon, and, yep, cucumber.

The Sankt Gallen Brewery, in Atsugi-shi, Japan, once produced a special chocolate stout called Un, Kono Kuro, which is made with Black Ivory coffee beans. So far, so good, but please be aware: the coffee beans were digested first by elephants at Thailand's Golden Triangle Elephant Foundation.

The Wynkoop Brewing Company, in Denver, Colorado, USA, has created an unusual beer, to say the least. Rocky Mountain Oyster Stout contains a very special ingredient—freshly sliced and roasted bull's testicles (three balls per barrel, to be precise).

Fossil Fuels Brewing Company, in Manteca, California, USA, has made a very, very old beer indeed, using ancient yeast extracted from amber. Microbiologist Dr. Raul Cano extracted 2,000 microorganisms from amber dated at around 25 to 45 million years old, including yeast strains that resemble the modern yeast used in brewing and baking. From this, the brewery managed to create an ancient-yeast beer, AY 108.

Sapporo Breweries, in Tokyo, Japan, launched a rather special, limited-edition beer on December 3, 2009. Sapporo's Space Barley contained malt that had been made from the offspring of barley seeds, which had undertaken a five-month space flight on the International Space Station in 2006.

On a similar note, Celest-Jewel Ale by Dogfish Head Brewery, in Milton, Delaware, USA, is made with crushed dust from lunar meteorites. Apparently, the moon dust contains minerals and salts that help with fermentation.

The Seefurth family's *Mamma Mia Pizza Beer* includes a margherita pizza in the mash—that's right, an ale brewed with oregano, basil, tomato, and garlic. Mmm…

SOME BEER RECORD-BREAKERS!

The most bottles of beer opened in one minute using a chainsaw is 24. This feat was achieved by Ashrita Furman in New York, USA, on May 3, 2016.

On June 5, 2013, Julia Gunthel (aka Zlata) took just one minute to open 8 beer bottles in Istanbul, Turkey. That sounds easy, you might say. However, bear in mind that Julia is a contortionist and opened the bottles with her feet while balancing on her elbows.

On June 22, 1977, Steven Petrosino of New Cumberland, Pennsylvania, USA, drank 33fl oz (1 liter) of beer in 1.3 seconds.

German, Michael Sturm carried 26 full beer steins in one go for 131ft 3in (40m) at the Oktoberfest Brahma Extra São Paulo, in Brazil, on September 27, 2017.

We all know that barmaids in Germany can carry a lot of beer. Anita Schwarz secured the female world record for carrying the most beer steins— 19 in all—over a distance of 131ft 3in (40m) in Mesenich, Germany, on November 9, 2008.

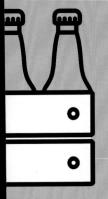

Art out of beer crates? Well, the largest beer-crate sculpture ever created used 4,734 crates. This amazing construction was built by German Feuerwehr Feldhausen on January 17, 2015. The sculpture was of a fire truck.

Okay, so beer mats are usually small pieces of card, right? Wrong. The world's largest beer mat measured 49ft 3in (15m) in diameter and was 2.36in (6cm) thick. It was created by the Carlsberg brewery, in Denmark, on September 15, 2002.

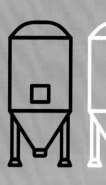

What is it with beer mats? On July 12, 2006, Englishman Dean Gould managed to catch 402 beer mats in one hand that were stacked on his elbow—in one go.

In 2006, Swiss brewery Valaisanne built the world's tallest tabletop beer dispenser. The huge dispenser is 9ft 10in (3m) tall and has been put on display in Sion, Switzerland.

The largest pub crawl involved 4,885 participants who visited 10 pubs in Kansas City's Power and Light District, in Missouri, USA. The event was organized by Crawl for Cancer on June 1, 2013. In all, the revelers visited a total of 21 different bars and were dressed in an array of crazy costumes.

Fancy being a bartender? The shifts can be long, but probably not as long as the marathon effort put in by Ruth Brands at the Café Het Gildenhuis, in Opglabbeek, Belgium. Ruth worked solidly behind the bar from October 30 to November 4, 2012—that's 111 hours!

The world's longest beer garden was created by Präsenta GmbH and the Internationale Berliner Bierfestival, in Berlin, Germany, on August 7, 2011. It measures 5,971ft 1in (1,820m).

BEER BUFFS
AND GEEKS

Experts estimate that the global beer market was worth nearly $600 billion in 2015, with forecasts suggesting this figure will continue to rise each year.

The world's largest beer festival is Oktoberfest. Held annually in Munich, Germany, it is a 16-day fair that runs from late September to the first weekend in October. More than 6 million people from around the world attend each year. Oktoberfest originally took place on October 12, 1810, to celebrate the marriage of Crown Prince Ludwig of Bavaria to Princess Therese von Sachsen-Hildburghausen. Total beer consumption at this annual event usually reaches around 1,700,000 US gallons (6,500,000 liters).

Oktoberfest might be the world's biggest beer festival, but the Great American Beer Festival held every September, in Denver, Colorado, USA, gives it a close run for its money. In 2017, the festival was attended by 800 US breweries and served over 3,900 different American beers.

There are breweries large and small, but one of the criteria for categorizing them is the volume of beer that they produce per year. So, here's the low-down:

❖ Microbreweries   Up to 15,000 barrels
❖ Regional breweries   15,000 to 2,000,000 barrels
❖ Larger breweries   More than 2,000,000 barrels

Bragdy Gwynant, in Capel Bangor, Aberystwyth, Wales, UK, is the smallest commercial brewery in the world, producing just 10.8 US gallons (40.9 liters) per batch—solely for the adjacent Tynllidiart Arms.

The longest recorded hangover is said to have lasted one month after a Scotsman consumed 60 pints (35 liters) of beer over four days in 2006, resulting in a long-lasting headache and blurred vision— I should say so!

There are many theories to explain the "33" that appears on the back of every bottle of Rolling Rock beer. One suggestion is that it was originally a printer's error, with the "33" actually referring to the number of words that appeared in the beer's slogan. No one knows for sure, but, such was the intrigue generated by the mystery, that the company left the "33" on the label.

Beer buffs like to do things properly, not being content with just pouring their beer into any old glass. Different types of glass can be used to enhance a beer's flavor, color, and aroma. These are the main glass types for the beer connoisseur:

❖ Pint glass
❖ Beer mug
❖ Beer stein
❖ Goblet and chalice
❖ Pilsner glass
❖ Weizen
❖ Snifter
❖ Tulip and thistle glass
❖ IPA glass
❖ Stange glass
❖ Tasting and sampler glasses (for the real beer buffs)

TOP 10
Strongest Beers

1 Brewmeister's
Snake Venom
67.5% ABV

Each bottle has a label stating:
*"This beer is strong.
Do not exceed 35ml in one sitting."*

You have been warned!

2 Brouwerij't Koelschip's
Start the Future
60% ABV

3 Schorschbräu's
*Schorschbock 57% Finis
Coronat Opus*
57.7% ABV

4 BrewDog's
The End of History
55% ABV

Only 12 bottles of this beer were made, with each presented inside a dead animal that the brewery claimed was roadkill.

5 Schorschbräu's
Schorschbock 43%
43.4% ABV

6 BrewDog's
Sink the Bismarck
41% ABV

7 Baladin's
Esprit de Nöel
40% ABV

8 De Struise Brouwers'
*Black Damnation
VI–Messy*
39% ABV

9 Revelation Cat
Craft Brewery's
Freeze the Penguin
35% ABV

10 BrewDog's
Tactical Nuclear Penguin
32% ABV

NOW FOR THE SCIENCE BIT...

Historians believe that hops were originally added to beer over 2,000 years ago, not to add flavor, but because of their antiseptic properties; they reduced fungal and other infections. Adding hops meant brewers did not have to achieve a high-alcohol content to protect their beer from spoilage. As a result, they could use fewer barley grains and therefore make more profit!

Beer helped the 18th-century scientist-clergyman Joseph Priestley in his investigations into gases. In 1767, Priestley began a ministry in Leeds, England, near a brewery. On visiting the brewery, Priestley noticed a dense gas—that is, carbon dioxide—hanging over the large fermentation vats. This led him to develop a method for infusing liquids with carbon dioxide by placing a bowl of water above the vat of fermenting beer, thus producing the first-ever soda water.

Louis Pasteur, the 19th-century Frenchman who invented pasteurization as a means of killing bacteria in foodstuffs such as milk, initially made his famous discovery of bacteria while studying beer. Pasteur realized that the beer was alive with bacteria, so paving the way for the germ theory of disease and modern medicinal hygiene.

Dark glass bottles keep out light better, which helps prevent beers going bad or being "lightstruck"— you don't want a "skunked" beer.

Although the technology for canning beer had been available for a few decades, it wasn't until late 1933 that the American Can Company managed to persuade the Gottfrieg Kreuger Brewing Company, in New Jersey, USA, to trial beer in cans. The 2,000 trial cans were known as Krueger's Special Beer. Taking a commercial gamble, two types of canned beer, Krueger's Finest Beer and Krueger's Cream Ale, were eventually released for sale on January 24, 1935.

If you stick your fingers in the foamy head of a glass of beer, the foam will disperse. This is because naturally occurring oils in your skin break the surface tension of the bubbles and make them collapse.

Did you know that there are male and female hop flowers? Well, brewers only use female hops to make beer, as the male hops don't taste very nice!

Researchers at Stanford University, California, USA, have discovered that beer bubbles create a gravity-defying loop. Studies revealed that bubbles move up the center of the glass, where there is less frictional drag, and then down the outside of the glass as the top of the beer becomes crowded.

There is an alcoholic cloud in space! British scientists used radio telescopes to study an interstellar gas cloud of ethyl alcohol and worked out that it contains enough alcohol to make 400 trillion trillion pints of beer. The cloud, which is located in the Aquila constellation, has a less-than-catchy name, G34.3, and is approximately 10,000 light years away.

Don't lie your beer bottles down in the refrigerator. Always keep them upright to minimize oxidation and contamination from the cap.

The aroma compounds produced by common brewer's yeast help to give beer its distinctive smell. The aroma apparently has an evolutionary purpose: to attract fruit flies so that they can disperse the yeast cells. In this symbiotic arrangement, the flies feed on the yeasts and the yeasts benefit from the movement of the flies.

On airplanes, cabin conditions like air pressure, oxygen levels, and humidity can affect your sense of taste. That's why Cathay Pacific has introduced a special beer for air travel. Betsy Beer is sweeter than your average beer, using honey and longan fruit to offset the bitter flavors that are amped up in the air, and more highly carbonated, to counteract the numbing of the senses experienced on board.

TOP 10
Expensive Beers

1 Nail Brewing's
Antarctic Nail Ale
$1,850/500ml bottle

2 Cantillon's
Loerik 1998
$2,583/750ml bottle

3 BrewDog's
The End of History
$765/330ml bottle

4 De Cam and
Drie Fonteinen's
Millennium Geuze 1998
$923/750ml bottle

5 The Lost Abbey's
Cable Car Kriek
$923/750ml bottle

6 Carlsberg's
Jacobsen Vintage No.1
$400/375ml bottle

7 Crown's
Ambassador's Reserve
$90–800/750ml bottle

8 Schorschbräu's
Schorschbock 57
$275/330ml bottle

Only 30 individually labeled bottles of this beer were made, using thawed Antarctic ice, in association with the Sea Shepherd Conservation Society, an organization dedicated to protecting the world's oceans. At auction, Bottle 1 sold for $800. Bottle 2 sold for an eye-watering $1,850.

9 Samuel Adams'
Utopias
$200/750ml bottle

10 BrewDog's
Sink the Bismarck
$80/375ml bottle

[ARRANGED BY PRICE/ML.
MOST OF THESE BEERS WERE LIMITED-
RELEASE ONLY AND SOLD AT AUCTION
TO THE HIGHEST BIDDER]

Beer for Body and Soul

Often referred to as "liquid bread" due to its nutritional content, beer can have health benefits when drunk in moderation.

Beer contributes to strong bones: Beer contains silicon, a chemical element that increases the calcium deposits and minerals necessary for maintaining healthy bone tissue.

Beer reduces the risk of kidney stones: A study published in the *American Journal of Epidemiology* estimated that consuming a bottle of beer every day reduces the risk of developing stones by 40 percent.

Beer improves cognitive function: The *New England Journal of Medicine* studied women who consume a moderate amount of beer and found that they had better cognitive function than nondrinkers.

Beer is good for heart health: This is because alcohol raises the levels of HDL (that's good cholesterol) associated with a lower risk of cardiovascular problems.

Beer contains B vitamins and antioxidants:
B vitamins are important for cell health, while the antioxidants in beer are probably more easily absorbed than they are from wine, for example.

Fancy a spa with a difference? Why not try a beer spa in the Czech Republic, where you can literally bathe in warm lager, with hop flowers, brewer's yeast, and herbs added for their health benefits—these include improved circulation, skin exfoliation, and purification. You can have a drink while you're in there, too. The Chodovar brewery and Bernard Beer Spa both come highly recommended.

Hops have lots of health benefits, supposedly helping with joint inflammation, insomnia, respiratory spasms, and indigestion.

MORE BEER RECORD-BREAKERS

Fancy learning a good party trick? Then try emulating Ashrita Furman's mind-blowing achievement—he balanced 81 pint-sized beer glasses on his chin for 12.10 seconds in his backyard in Jamaica, New York, USA, on August 12, 2007.

The highest number of glasses of beer pulled in one hour is 1,437, a feat accomplished by German Achim Gratias, in Hürtgenwald, Germany, on June 27, 2006.

Or how about balancing 235 pint-sized beer glasses on your head for 13 seconds? That is what John Evans did in Dassau, Germany, on September 7, 2002.

he highest beer
eg toss for a female
12ft 10in (3.9m)
y Ukrainian Nina
eria, in Rome,
aly, on March 12,
012. Go girl!

Murali K.C removed a total of 68 beer-bottle caps with his teeth in just one minute. This was achieved at Country Club Mysore, in Bangalore, India, on September 17, 2011. Ouch!

he highest beer keg toss for a male is 26ft .93in (8.05m) by Icelander Thor Björnsson, in Milan, Italy, on July 11, 2014. The beer keg weighed in at 27lb (12.32kg).

The largest collection of beer labels belongs to German Hendrik Thomann. The count on October 3, 2012, revealed that Hendrik had collected 548,567 different beer labels (with 173,324 originating from Germany alone).

American, Ron Werner owns the largest collection of beer bottles. As of January 27, 2012, Ron had managed to accumulate a total of 25,866 bottles. That's about 1,000 bottles a year since the age of 14.

The largest collection of beer mats belongs to Leo Pisker from Langenzersdorf, Austria. Amazingly, Leo has amassed 152,860 beer mats from 192 different countries.

Meraner Altstadtvereinigung, from Merano, Italy, created the world's largest beer tankard. It is 19ft 3in (5.87m) tall and has a diameter of 6ft 7.92in (2.03m). Not surprisingly, the tankard can hold a lot of beer— 3,410 US gallons (12,910 liters) to be precise.

On July 6, 2014, Angus Wood and Ed Dupuy of Stod Fold Brewing Company, in Halifax, UK, poured the world's largest glass of beer. It took one hour to fill the glass with 550 US gallons (2,082 liters) of beer.

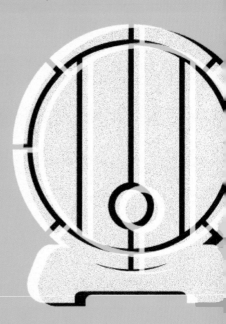

Some folk are devoted to beer. As of January 29, 2014, Englishman Bruce Masters had visited 46,495 pubs and bars since 1960. And still counting...

ACKNOWLEDGMENTS

Thanks as ever to Cindy Richards and Pete Jorgensen, and the rest of the wonderful team at CICO books, for asking me to write another fact- and fun-filled book. Special thanks, of course, go to the brilliant designer, Mark Latter, with whom I have worked happily and creatively for more years than I dare say. I've discovered some incredible and downright weird facts about beer and brewing, while digging deep into the archaeological archives and exploring the endless rabbit-holes of the Internet. As much as possible, the facts have been verified across a range of sources. I would especially like to thank en.wikipedia.org (and its many contributors), www.dumblaws.com, and also Guinness World Records (www.guinnessworldrecords.com) for their beer-related records. For the fascinating statistics on global beer consumption on page 13, I'd like to credit Kirin Holdings Company (www.kirinholdings.co.jp).

Picture Credits:
Images sourced from shutterstock.com and istockphoto.com.

Cheers!